Endorsements

"Women love inspiration to use alongside reading God's Word, and I am no exception! Thank you for opening your heart to share ways in which the Lord has worked in your life from the shores of Galilee to the heart of Tennessee and for weaving through these pages your own personal memories from the generations of your own family. Your wisdom, coupled with a reminder to BEHOLD and focus on the Savior, unfolds to feed a hungry soul in any season of life!"

—Dorothy Kelley Patterson, professor of theology,
Southwestern Baptist Theological Seminary, Fort Worth, TX

"Joyce Rogers loves the Lord and His Word. What a joy it is to read Behold! as it expounds on gazing upon the Lord's steadfast love for us. Through sharing insights from her vast life experience as well as her love for wonderful hymns of the faith, Joyce leads us to the throne of grace. Let us seek to truly behold His glory by meditating on His unchanging Word and claiming His precious promises. This devotional will encourage you to do just that."

—Mrs. R. Albert Mohler, Jr. (Mary), director of Seminary Wives
Institute, Southern Baptist Theological Seminary, Louisville, KY

"Joyce Rogers has the unique gift of expressing her faith with simplicity, yet depth. In this devotional, she takes the word Behold! and gives it a biblical context, a thorough explanation, as well as fresh personal application. You will be encouraged and blessed by this book!"

—Susie Hawkins, author, speaker, member of Flourish Team
(ministry of North American Mission Board)

"This devotional book will be one that you will want to read over and over again. Thank you, Mrs. Joyce for taking the reader on a journey of inspirational scripture, amazing hymns, and heart-stirring poetry. I loved being taken back to Jerusalem in my mind through your creative writings. Thank you for the reminder that as we study God's Word, we should never just 'glance' at His Word, but we must 'gaze' upon every word as He guides and comforts us along life's path. May we always 'behold' His glory."

—Rhonda Sinquefield, wife, mother, Sunday school teacher

"Joyce has spent much of her life 'looking to Jesus,' and in this book, she has compiled a beautiful selection of scripture and devotional thoughts to help us 'Behold' Him with awe and wonder."

—Vonette Bright, co-founder Campus Crusade for Christ

Behold!

Devotional Glimpses of Precepts, People, and Places of the Lord

Joyce Rogers

Published by
Innovo Publishing, LLC
www.innovopublishing.com
1-888-546-2111

Providing Full-Service Publishing Services for
Christian Authors, Artists & Organizations: Hardbacks, Paperbacks,
eBooks, Audiobooks, Music & Film

BEHOLD:
Devotional Glimpses of Precepts, People, and Places of the Lord
Copyright © 2014 Innovo Publishing

Scripture taken from the New King James Version®. Copyright © 1982
by Thomas Nelson, Inc. Used by permission. All rights reserved.
Scripture marked KJV taken from the King James Version.

Library of Congress Control Number: 2014940660
ISBN 13: 978-1-61314-202-8

Cover Design & Interior Layout: Innovo Publishing, LLC

Printed in the United States of America
U.S. Printing History

First Edition: July 2014

Dedication

I dedicate this book to my greatest prayer partner, my sister—Doris Swaringen. She is always praising the Lord and *beholding Him*. She considers it her highest ministry to pray for others. I am so very privileged that she always prays for me. I love you so much, my sweet sister!

I also dedicate this book to my long-time and precious friend, Mary Buckner, who helped me in the Children's New Members' Class at Bellevue Baptist Church for fifteen out of the thirty-four years I taught it. She went to be with Jesus in October of 2013. I have many sweet memories of talking and singing with Mary about heaven and reading the scriptures that tell about its wonders.

I also want to mention my wonderful husband, Adrian, whom I have loved since I was but a child. He spent his entire life "lifting up Jesus" and pleading with others to "Come to Jesus." He taught me more than anyone else to love Jesus and to *behold* Him every day of my life.

In Appreciation

Most of all, I want to give honor to my Lord and Savior, Jesus Christ, Who gave His all for me. I also want to express my deep appreciation to my editor, Darya Crockett, who was so very helpful in her corrections and suggestions; to Terry Bailey for her guidance through the whole process; to Bart Dahmer, who believed in my book enough to publish it; to my sister, Doris Swaringen and my good friend Elizabeth Griffin, who read my original manuscript before I even thought about it becoming a book and who have loved me unconditionally; to Audrey Davis, who read my manuscript and caught some corrections that needed to be made; and to my children, Steve and David Rogers, Gayle Foster, and Janice Edmiston, who read my manuscript and were so encouraging to me.

Much love because of Him,

Joyce

Contents

Unless otherwise noted, all poetry in this book
was written by Joyce Rogers.

The magnificent sunrise pictured on the cover of this
book was taken by Joyce one morning during her
quiet time with the Lord. It was this very sunrise
that inspired her to write the book, *Behold!*

Preface

The word *behold* means to gaze upon, not just to glance at. It has been an exciting adventure to find numerous places in God's Word where *behold* appears. In this book, I will share with you some personal experiences and devotional thoughts that contain the word *behold* centered around some of the precepts, people, and places of the Lord. I hope they will be a blessing to you as they have been to me.

Mainly, I want you to *behold* Jesus. He wants to change your life. Come, let us kneel before the Lord, our Maker, for it is here that we can best *behold* Him. Indeed, "it is enough to see Jesus, and to go on seeing Him."[1] In times when I have come to the end of myself, I have truly *seen* Him.

---

[1] Roy Hession and Revel Hession, *We Would See Jesus* (Ft. Washington, PA: CLC Ministries, 2005).

Chapter 1

"*Behold*, I long for Your precepts;"
(Psalm 119:40)

Psalm 119 is the longest chapter in the Bible. It has 176 verses. The theme of this chapter is "the Word of God." The phrase "according to Your word" echoes over and over again. The question asked in verse 9 is, "How can a young man cleanse his way?" The answer follows, "By taking heed according to Your word." A number of prayers are offered "according to Your word."

> "Revive me *according to Your word*" (Psalm 119:25).

> "Strengthen me *according to Your word*" (Psalm 119:28).

> "Let Your mercies come also to me, O LORD—Your salvation *according to Your word*" (Psalm 119:41).

"Let, I pray, Your merciful kindness be my comfort, *According to Your word* to Your servant" (Psalm 119:76).

"Uphold me *according to Your word,* that I may live . . ." (Psalm 119:116).

"Give me understanding *according to Your word*" (Psalm 119:169b).

"Deliver me *according to Your word*" (Psalm 119:170).

A variety of words is used to describe the Word of God in Psalm 119:

> Your word
> The law of the Lord
> His testimonies
> Your statutes
> Your commandments
> Your precepts
> Your judgments
> Your ordinances

There is a blessing pronounced on those who *keep* His testimonies. There is a positive response given by the psalmist over and over again: "I will . . ."

"*I will* keep Your statutes" (Psalm 119:8).

"*I will* meditate on Your precepts" (Psalm 119:15, 78).

"*I will* delight myself in Your statutes . . ." (Psalm 119:16a, 47).

"*I will* keep Your precepts with my whole heart" (Psalm 119:69).

"*I will* consider Your testimonies" (Psalm 119:95b).

I love the Word of God. It has been my guide and comfort since my youth. I love to do word studies. When my beloved Adrian went home to be with Jesus, I studied the concepts of heaven, grace, mercy, peace, help, and hope. I studied God's Old Testament names, especially the name of God for widows, Jehovah Sabaoth, which means "the Lord of hosts." I circled every reference to this name. I "claimed" this name many times and asked Him to fight my battles for me. What a blessing this habit has brought to my life!

My current study is on the word *behold*. It has been replaced in the more modern versions with the words *see* or *listen*. I do not believe these words sufficiently convey the meaning of *behold* because it means to gaze upon, not just to glance at. It has been an exciting and blessed adventure to find numerous places in God's Word where *behold* appears.

Chapter 2

"*Behold*, the LORD our God . . ."

"Behold, the LORD our God has shown us His glory and His greatness" (Deuteronomy 5:24).

"Hear, O Israel: The LORD our God, the LORD is one!" (Deuteronomy 6:4).

Behold, there is *one God*,
I shall bow to no other;
Jesus said, "I and my Father are one" (John 10:30).
There is *one sacrifice* for sins forever (Hebrews 10:12).
Jesus cried out on the cross, "It is finished!" (John 19:30).

There is *one Mediator* between God and man (1 Timothy 2:5),
The man, Christ Jesus, seated at the Father's right hand,
Praying for you and me.
Jesus prayed that we may be one (John 17:10),
One with Him—one with the Father and the Holy Spirit;
One with each other, even as He and the Father were one.

There is one Lord—
Every knee shall bow to Him and every tongue
confess that Jesus Christ is Lord! (Philippians 2:10).

One faith—
Jesus is the Author and Finisher
of our faith (Hebrews 12:2).

One baptism—
Jesus identified with us,
became sin for us (Romans 6:4).

One body—
If we are in Christ, we are a part of His body;
and He is the Head (Ephesians 1:22).

One Spirit—
The Holy Spirit, Who is Jesus living in us,
leading us into all truth (John 16:13).

Chapter 3

"*Behold*, it was very good."
(Genesis 1:31, KJV)

In the first six days of creation, God stepped back to observe what He had made and said, "It is good." But at the end of the sixth day, he beheld *all* that He had created and said, "It is *very* good!" What beauty there must have been there in the Garden of Eden—what perfection!

I've seen some of the beautiful gardens of the world. I still remember gazing down from a window in an ancient castle in Gruyere, Switzerland, and observing the formal garden below, immaculately kept and perfectly trimmed. I called for Adrian to come and see it with me. Something beautiful should always be shared.

I haven't seen *all* of the gardens of the world. Some can no longer be seen but only remembered, like the hanging gardens of Babylon. However, the most beautiful garden that I have seen is Buchart Gardens in Victoria, Canada—fifty acres of breathtaking beauty.

The sunken garden, which was originally a cement quarry, is still etched in my mind. Mr. Buchart was a cement magnate and when the quarry was left empty, his wife, who had a love affair with plants and flowers from around the world, created the magnificent sunken garden as well as the rest of the grounds. Their grandchildren now maintain the gardens.

I was there in August when the roses and the begonias were at their peak—simply gorgeous! I've never seen such giant begonias, hanging in baskets that displayed their variety and glorious colors. Even the parking lots are more beautiful, with multicolored splendor, than most gardens. I have been there five times—four with my beloved, Adrian.

It is one place in the world that is worth "beholding" over and over again. If this beauty still remains after the fall of mankind into sin, I'm sure we can't imagine the *original* splendor.

I am also a connoisseur of beautiful sunrises and sunsets around the world. When I traveled to the Holy Land with Adrian and groups of friends, I loved to rise very early to see the sunrise over the Sea of Galilee. However, there has never been a sunset that ever could compare to the one I saw at Calvary. I can hardly describe the 160-degree sunset that lasted for an hour when Adrian and I were in the Bahamas. We *beheld* and *beheld*.

Today, as I was having my quiet time with the Lord, one of the most beautiful sunrises I have ever seen blazed across the entire sky. I tried to capture it on my iPhone, but it was impossible. Lord, the magnificence of Your artistic splendor is beyond compare. "Behold, it was very good"!

Behold, a Glorious Gift

Right outside my window
behold
the beauty of the sunrise
blazed across the sky.
What wonder
What glory!
A gift—a gracious gift
to carry with me
throughout the day!
You stroked the sky with glorious splendor—
A reminder of the greatness
of my Creator God!
What magnificence for so short a time.
But for all who were up to greet
the Lord this morning
He gave a glorious gift—
Thank You! Thank You! Thank You!
—Your loving daughter, Joyce

Chapter 4

"*Behold,* the bush was burning . . ."

(Exodus 3:2)

". . . behold the bush was burning with fire, but the bush was not consumed" (Exodus 3:2).

Our Arab guide, Saad, had taken us out into the Shepherds' Field in Bethlehem. He set fire to a bush—a random bush—and it burned a long time. Our group stood around and sang, "We are standing on holy ground."[2] Could it have been a bush like this that Moses "happened upon"—that he saw burning but not consumed? "Our" bush was not a miracle but an illustration—a remembrance of Moses' bush.

After getting his attention with this phenomenon, God called to Moses from the burning bush and reminded him of His holiness. He said, "Do not draw

---

[2] Geron Davis, "Holy Ground," © 1983 by Meadowgreen Music Company/Songchannel Music Company/ASCAP (adm. By EMI CMG Publishing). All rights reserved.

near this place. Take your sandals off your feet, for the place where you stand is holy ground" (Exodus 3:5).

Before God can use you or me, we must stand in awe of His presence. Too many Christian leaders have caught a glimpse of *their* importance, not of the glory of *His* presence. Moses spent forty years on the backside of the desert learning humility. The Bible says that Moses was the meekest man who ever lived. Yes, God *does* want to use you and me. We may have to spend some time on the backside of the desert before He can.

May the story of the burning bush remind us, first of all, that God wants to get our attention. But most of all, He wants us to recognize His presence. As Major Ian Thomas observed, "Any old bush will do" if we allow God to set our hearts on fire. Oh, may we keep burning for Him—lingering to *behold* His presence and then to go forth to set the world on fire for His glory, not ours!

Could You Use Me?

A princess heard a baby cry
and Pharaoh's kingdom fell;
Mary heard a baby cry
and He saved my soul from hell.

Despise not little things—
They're part of God's eternal plan;

He chose the weak, the base, despised
to bring His glory down to man.

Lord, could You use me?
I'm no one great;
There are few who even know my name.
I'm not able,
but I'm willing
to let You fill me and
tell others why You came.

Are You sure You want to use me, Lord?
Yes, I'll go wherever You direct,
obey whatever You command.

I'm available to bring Your glory down to man.

Chapter 5

"*Behold*, I create Jerusalem . . . a joy."
(Isaiah 65:18b)

Jerusalem brought joy to the very heart of God. Isaiah 65:18b says, "For behold, I create Jerusalem as a rejoicing, and her people a joy." Jerusalem became the capital city of the Jewish kingdom under David. His son, Solomon, built the first temple there. Jerusalem is still the most important city in the world.

I have visited this city on numerous occasions. The anticipation of *beholding* this city was so great the first time we rode into the city. We sang that great hymn, "We're marching to Zion, beautiful, beautiful Zion. We're marching upward to Zion, the beautiful city of God." I felt a thrill when I first caught a glimpse of the ancient wall that surrounds Old Jerusalem.

Yes, Jerusalem is called "the city of God." Psalm 87:3 says, "Glorious things are spoken of you, O city of God!" Psalm 48 tells of the wonders of Jerusalem, also calling it the city of God. There is a song based on Psalm

48:1, and I love to sing it, especially when I have been in Jerusalem.

God has promised to establish this city forever. Psalm 48:8 says, "As we have heard, So we have seen In the city of the LORD of hosts, In the city of our God: God will establish it forever. Selah."

I love the popular Israeli song, "Jerusalem of Gold"[3] whose chorus is:

> Jerusalem, Jerusalem
> O city with a heart of gold
> My heart shall sing your praise forever
> Jerusalem!

Adrian and I have stayed many times in the Five Arches Hotel on the Mount of Olives. I loved to rise very early to see the sunrise over the old city of Jerusalem, surrounded by its ancient wall.

Indeed, it was a thrill to see the city splashed with the wonder of the sunrise. There were olive trees and beautiful roses in the garden in front of the hotel. I have tried to capture these moments with artistic photography. Yes, if you rise early to see the sunrise, you will experience *Jerusalem of gold.*

Jesus visited this city many times. He wept over this city and cried out, "O Jerusalem, Jerusalem . . . how

---

[3] Naomi Shemer, "Jerusalem of Gold," 1967.

often would I have gathered thy children together, even as a hen gathereth her chicks under her wings, and ye would not!" (Matthew 23:37, KJV).

A Panorama of Old Jerusalem

I sit upon the Mount of Olives
and scan the view before my eyes;
A panorama of Old Jerusalem
Down before me lies.

From here I can almost hear the Savior weeping,
Oh Jerusalem, I long to hold you in my keeping.
Looking across the Kidron Valley
I catch a glimpse of the Eastern Gate;
Where the Lord on donkey lowly
Entered at God's appointed date.

Beyond this lies the Temple courtyard
Where Jesus often taught,
Not one stone lies upon another now
As He said, "'Twould come to naught."

Descending a dusty pathway
I enter the Garden where He prayed;
I walk among the olive trees
Where on His face He laid.

He went from loud Hosannas
To a cross upon a hill;
Still some praise Him with their lips
But refuse to do His will.

From this Mount He ascended
To His Father up above;
He's seated in the heavenlies
Interceding through His love.

One day His feet will touch
Upon this Mount again;
From Mount Zion on King David's throne
He'll justly rule and reign.

Those of us who know Him
Will come with Him to share
The glories of His matchless love
His tenderness and care.

We'll know His presence,
A thousand perfect years we'll
Rule and walk with Him;
Then heaven will come down to earth
As the New Jerusalem!

There will be special mention of those who are born there. Psalm 87:5–6 says, "And of Zion it will be said, 'This one and that one were born in her; And the Most High Himself shall establish her.' The LORD will record, When He registers the peoples: 'This one was born there.' Selah."

Why Is Jerusalem So Special?

In Old Testament times, the king resided there at Mount Zion. The Temple, the place of worship for the Jewish people, was there. It was outside the city walls of Jerusalem where Jesus was crucified, buried, and rose again. It will be to the Mount of Olives in Jerusalem where Jesus will come back again.

There's something that draws you there. The city is replete with history, with underground tunnels, with intrigue. The ruins of the ancient city beckon you:

> to discover their meaning
> to remember the stories of their past
> to challenge you to study the Savior's life
> to trust His death and resurrection for your salvation

Constantly, new ruins are being excavated and new discoveries found. The Orthodox Jews are digging near the site where they believe the ancient Temple stood.

Some even believe that the Ark of the Covenant, which has been lost since ancient times, will one day be discovered there. The Orthodox Jews are even preparing furniture like the originals to go inside a newly built temple.

Jerusalem Day

Much controversy surrounds this city. Wars have been fought for its possession. In modern times the Jewish people celebrate Jerusalem Day—when the city was again united in 1967. I have been there on this day and seen the people flock there to go to the Western Wall to celebrate. The wall is the last remains of anything to do with the ancient Temple that was destroyed in AD 70 by the Romans.

On Mount Zion is the burial place of King David. I have been there and witnessed the Jewish people file by to pay honor to him. Every guest must wear a head covering as they pass by the burial place of David.

A City of Great Contrast

Jerusalem is a city of great contrast. There is the old city and the new city. I have been to both. The new city of Jerusalem holds the Knesset Building, which is Israel's main government building. There is a giant replica of a menorah like the one that was in the Temple, which is the symbol of the modern nation of Israel. The museum, The Shrine of the Book, which contains the ruins of the Dead Sea Scrolls and other ancient items found with them, is a must see. The Isaiah scroll is featured in the museum. You can Google The Shrine of the Book and find a sixty-second tour of the museum.

A walk down the streets of old Jerusalem seems like a walk back into time with its smells and sights. I can see it all in my mind's eye. I have loved taking pictures and videos, trying to capture the "flavor" of these sights.

You can ride a camel or a donkey for only a few dollars. You can buy a "crown of thorns," woven from a thorn bush in Jerusalem. I purchased a Persian rug in the old city of Jerusalem. The fact that I purchased it in Jerusalem gives it great value to me. Everyone who goes there comes back with souvenirs. I purchased an olive wood bowl filled with olive wood "eggs." I have candlestick holders that decorate my breakfast room that were purchased in the hotel on the Mount of Olives.

The Woman at the Wall

When we first visited the Western Wall in Jerusalem, I was fascinated by a woman praying at the wall. I took her picture and wrote this poem:

The Woman at the Wall

God, are You here, here at this Wall
Are You nearer here than any other place?
I write my prayer and fold it and place it
Here between these cracks and ask,
"God are You here, here at this Wall?"

"Yes, my child, I'm here, here at this Wall
But not nearer here than any other place.
I'm anywhere you breathe the name of Jesus!"

What Jesus Did for Me There

Of all the sights, sounds, and places of renown
that I have experienced in Jerusalem, my favorite places
are Gordon's Calvary and the Empty Tomb. I've been
privileged to climb this hill on several occasions. It is
covered with rocks and giant thorns. To me, these are
reminders that this is still the place of death and a curse.
Just think, Jesus took my curse and your curse on the
cross, somewhere on that hill. At the foot of Calvary,
there is a bus station. People come and go as if nothing
significant ever happened here. It reminds me of the
scripture, "Is it nothing to you, all you who pass by?"
(Lamentations 1:12).

I loved stepping inside the Empty Tomb, which was near Skull Hill. I think about the resurrection and sing that simple but profound chorus[4]:

> He is Lord, He is Lord!
> He is risen from the dead
> and He is Lord.
> Every knee shall bow;
> ev'ry tongue confess that
> Jesus Christ is Lord!

There is a lovely garden there and the Empty Tomb is the center of it. It was here that we partook of the Lord's Supper and drank from olive wood cups. I like to meditate on His blood that was shed for me. I do not worship spots and places. If these are not the historical places, they help remind me of the love—the sacrifice—that was poured out for me at Calvary. They help remind me that He is alive forevermore. Hallelujah, what a Savior!

Next Year in Jerusalem!

The Jewish people love to say, "Next year in Jerusalem!" I have never tired of going to Jerusalem, but

---

[4] Author unknown, "He Is Lord."

I may have gone to this earthly city for the last time. Perhaps it will be "Next year in the *new* Jerusalem!"

Psalm 137:5–6 says, "If I forget you, O Jerusalem, Let my right hand forget its skill! If I do not remember you, Let my tongue cling to the roof of my mouth—If I do not exalt Jerusalem above my chief joy."

I can say along with the psalmist, "Our feet have been standing Within your gates, O Jerusalem" (Psalm 122:2). What an experience!

There is a command given in Psalm 122:6 that says, "Pray for the peace of Jerusalem: 'May they prosper who love you.'" Yes, I will and I do. I want to be obedient. And I know and love Jewish and Arab people who live there. I pray for them! Some of my Arab friends, who are also Christian brothers, are Saad, Philip, and Gabriel. A Jewish woman named Miriam stole my heart when she first became our guide over forty years ago.

Many times when Adrian and I have visited someone in the hospital, he has called on me to sing this scripture song:

> They that trust in the LORD shall be as mount Zion,
> which cannot removed, but abideth for ever.
> As the mountains are round about Jerusalem,
> so the LORD is round about his people
> from henceforth even for ever (Psalm 125:1–2, KJV).

Yes, I too love *Jerusalem of gold!*

Chapter 6

"*Behold*, I am vile;"

(Job 40:4)

Content to Know Who? To Know Him!

The first verse that came to my mind when my little baby Philip was snatched into heaven by sudden crib death was first uttered from the lips of Job: "The LORD gave, and the LORD has taken away; Blessed be the name of the LORD" (Job 1:21).

Throughout my life, Job has been one of my greatest comforters. He suffered unbearable pain and unexplainable loss, yet he refused to "curse God and die," as counseled by his wife (Job 2:9). Yes, Job has "been there." He understands *my* grief, *my* pain.

His declaration of faith in Job 13:15 to me is the greatest in all of God's Word. "Though He slay me, yet will I trust Him." I have borrowed his words to help me confess *my* faith in God.

But there was one flaw in his faith. He wanted an explanation. He wanted to know WHY. He cried out, "Oh that I knew where I might find Him" (Job. 23:3). It appears to be one of the most sublime statements in the Bible. However, the reason is not for fellowship, but for vindication. He said, "I would present my case before Him, And fill my mouth with arguments. . . . There the upright could reason with Him, And I would be delivered forever from my Judge" (Job 23:4, 7).

Job knew that he wasn't guilty of terrible sin like his friends proposed. But still his heart cried out, "Why? Why, why me, Lord?" He wanted desperately to find God and press his question—why?

Then finally God speaks. He had His own set of questions. First of all, there was the WHERE question.

> "WHERE were you when I laid the foundations of the earth? Tell Me, if you have understanding" (Job 38:4).

Then followed the WHO questions.

WHO marked off its dimensions?
    Surely you know!
WHO stretched a measuring line across it?
WHO laid its cornerstone?
WHO shut up the sea behind doors?

Then there were the YOU questions.

Have YOU ever given orders to the morning or shown the dawn its place?

Have YOU journeyed to the springs of the sea or walked in the recesses of the deep?

Have YOU seen the gates of the shadow of death?

Have YOU comprehended the vast expanses of the earth?

Tell me if YOU know all this.

On and on God interrogated Job and then asked one final question: "Shall the one who contends with the Almighty correct Him? He who rebukes God, let him answer it" (Job 40:2).

Then, oh then, Job answered the Lord, "Behold, I am vile; What shall I answer You? I lay my hand over my mouth. Once I have spoken, but I will not answer; Yes, twice, but I will proceed no further" (Job 40:4–5).

Then God questioned Job some more:

"Now prepare yourself like a man; I will question you, and you will answer Me" (Job. 40:7).

"Would you indeed annul My judgment? Would you condemn Me that you may be justified?" (Job 40:8).

"Who has preceded Me, that I should pay him? Everything under heaven is Mine" (Job 41:11).

Then, finally, Job replied:

"I have heard of You by the hearing of the ear, But now my eye sees You. Therefore I abhor myself, And repent in dust and ashes" (Job 42:5–6).

God never answered the *why* question. Job dropped that question when he, in awe and wonder, was confronted with the Almighty God. He was then content with the answer to the *who* question. He had encountered the living God, and it was enough!

Oh yes, I have received comfort from the words of Job. And I have been content to leave the *why* question with God. I have encountered the living God, and it is enough to see Him and to go on seeing Him. Yes, when I present myself before this awesome God, I too must confess, "Behold, I am vile; What shall I answer You? I lay my hand over my mouth" (Job 40:4).

Even if God had answered Job's *why* question, it would not have satisfied him. How could he possibly understand that God had allowed Satan to make a battlefield out of his life? But one day, we will all be gathered around the throne of God. We will rise to say, "Thank you, Job, for being faithful, for trusting God in the darkest night." Job has been one of my greatest counselors and comforters. Yes, it will be then that we'll understand!

Because of what I learned from Job, when loved ones whom I greatly treasured passed from my arms into His, I did not ask the question *why* but have been content to know *Who*—to know Him!

Chapter 7

"*Behold,* You desire truth . . ."

(Psalm 51:6)

My daddy's name is Guston C. Gentry. He built a successful business for thirty-five years. When he retired and sold his business, the people who bought it wanted to keep the name—Gentry Bros. Paint and Glass Co. You see, my daddy had a reputation for integrity. I'm so thankful that he passed that legacy on to me. Of course, I had to make the choice for myself, but I'm so grateful for his example.

As a young teenager, I was impacted greatly by a poem I read that was written by Edgar Guest. It began this way:

> I have to live with myself and so—
> I want to be fit for myself to know.

I wanted to live a life of integrity. Do you? Then tell Him so!

Then there is the concept of the *half*-truth. It means hedging on things—not an out and out lie, but a so-called acceptable *half*-truth. I was always taught that a *half*-truth was a *whole* lie. Weren't you?

Do you remember the story of Abraham, Sarah, and King Abimelech in the twentieth chapter of Genesis? Abraham and Sarah journeyed into the land of Gerar, where Abimelech was king. Sarah was beautiful, so to protect himself, Abraham told a half-truth and said that Sarah was his sister. He got her to participate in this half-truth also.

This half-truth—really a whole lie—almost got him, Sarah, the king, and all of his kingdom into big trouble. Abimelech took Sarah and was going to marry her, but God showed up in a dream and said, "Don't touch that woman. She's another man's wife. If you don't give her back, I'm going to kill you and all of your people" (Genesis 20:6–7, paraphrase). So he gave her back in a hurry and rebuked both of them. Just think about it, a pagan king rebuking God's man!

In this half-truth, Sarah was his father's daughter, but not the daughter of his mother. But he did not tell *all* of the truth—that she was indeed his wife.

I don't recommend engaging in telling half-truths. It could destroy your life. Do you want this scripture to be the prayer of your life instead?

"Vindicate me, O LORD, For I have walked in my integrity.
I have also trusted in the LORD; I shall not slip.
Examine me, O LORD, and prove me; Try my mind and my heart.
For Your lovingkindness is before my eyes, And I have walked in Your truth" (Psalm 26:1–3).

He promised,

"His truth shall be your shield and buckler" (Psalm 91:4).
". . . his truth endures to all generations" (Psalm 100:5).
"The works of His hands are verity (truth) and justice; All His precepts are sure. They stand fast forever and ever, And are done in truth and uprightness" (Psalm 111:7–8).
"The entirety of Your word is truth" (Psalm 119:160).
"The LORD is near to all who call upon Him . . . in truth" (Psalm 145:18).

Truth has many companions. God's Word tells about them:

> Light and truth (Psalm 43:3)
> Faithfulness and truth (Isaiah 25:1c)
> Mercy and truth (Psalm 85:10)

As I put on my spiritual armor, I make sure to buckle on the belt of truth, which is so essential and so foundational to all of my life. Yes, God's ways are true. His Word is true. I stand on His truth. Jesus is the way, the *truth*, and the life.

"I have chosen the way of truth" (Psalm 119:30a).

Chapter 8

"Behold, bless the LORD . . ."

(Psalm 134:1–2)

"Behold, bless the LORD,
All you servants of the LORD . . .
Lift up your hands in the sanctuary,
And bless the LORD" (Psalm 134:1–2).

I sing in my church's choir. On some occasions, I will lift my hands to praise and bless the Lord. My little baby Philip was taken to heaven by sudden crib death over fifty years ago. I knew that God's Word told me that I should "bless the Lord at all times," and to "give thanks in everything" (Psalm 34:1; 1 Thessalonians 5:18). I was trying to work these truths out in my life, but I didn't *feel* like praising God or thanking Him.

I did not want to be a hypocrite. One day I was reading Psalm 63 and stopped at verses 3 and 4:

"Because Your lovingkindness is better
than life, My lips shall praise You.
Thus I will bless You while I live;
I will lift up my hands in Your name."

Back in those days, no one in my denomination was lifting their hands to praise God. But there in my bedroom, all alone with God, I lifted my hands to Him and said, "No matter how I *feel*, by *faith* I will praise You!" I lifted my hands as an expression of my faith in Him.

I don't know how much longer it was, but one day I realized that I *felt* like praising God. I had learned how to *faith* my praise to God and wait for Him to give any feeling when He chose.

I am still praising God, sometimes lifting my hands to Him. Through the years, times of deep grief and sorrow and times of great joy have come my way. **Behold,** I will bless the Lord and lift my hands to Him!

What does it mean to me to lift my hands? It means that I recognize that God is present and that He is in control when everything is beyond my control. I lift up my hands to worship Him. It is an expression of my trust in Him when everything in my world is broken and I can't fix it.

Chapter 9

"*Behold*, You are there;"

(Psalm 139:8b)

"Whither shall I go from thy spirit? or whither shall I flee from thy presence? If I ascend up into heaven, thou art there: if I make my bed in hell, behold thou art there. If I take the wings of the morning, and dwell in the uttermost parts of the sea; Even there shall thy hand lead me, and thy right hand shall hold me" (Psalm 139:7–10, KJV).

We were in a large coliseum, sitting toward the very top. Our minister of career young people, Ken Whitten, was there with his wife and four young children. Little five-year-old Tara was busying herself. You would not have known that she was intently listening. The preacher then asked a rhetorical question, "Where is God?" He repeated with great emphasis, "*Where* is God?" Then little Tara called out, "I don't know, and don't ask me again!"

Psalm 139 answers this question. The answer is, *everywhere!* What comfort to know that when I am in the valley, He is there! When I am on the mountaintop, He is there! When I am in trouble, when days of sunshine come, praise the Lord, He is there, He is there! Oh, the promise of His presence is the greatest assurance of all! "Yea, though I walk through the valley of the shadow of death, I will fear no evil: for thou art with me . . ." (Psalm 23:4, KJV).

Above my bed is the inscription of my favorite Old Testament name for God—JEHOVAH SHAMMAH, which means, "The Lord is there!" Adrian didn't want to leave me, but God beckoned him home. Throughout my life, God's Word has whispered to my soul, "I'm there, my child, I'm there!"

When our baby Philip was snatched from my arms into the presence of Jesus through sudden crib death, God was there! He gave that assurance as I cried out to Him the words of the twenty-third Psalm: "For thou art with me; thy rod and thy staff they comfort me" (Psalm 23:4c, KJV).

> *God was there* when I miscarried three times—babies I longed for.
>
> *God was there* when my daughters, Gayle and Janice, my daughter-in-law, Kelly, and my granddaughter Angie miscarried their little ones.
>
> *God was there* when precious loved ones were left alone.

God was there when my life's companion,
whom I have loved since I was a child,
was taken to heaven.

God was there when I felt I must leave
beloved friends and comfortable
surroundings to follow God's
leadership.

God was there when my great-grandbaby,
Poppy Joy, left her mother's arms after
just several hours on this earth.

God was there through other heartaches
too personal to share.

Yes, He promised to never leave me nor forsake me (Hebrews 13:5). He has been faithful. He has kept His Word! He has also been there in the joyful times, and there have been many!

He was there in carefree school days filled
with challenge and fulfillment.

He was there at my wedding, when I
promised to love, cherish, and obey
that young man I had loved since I
was a child.

He was there at the births of our children—
each one so different and so special

(Steve, Gayle, David, Janice, and baby Philip)

He was there at five wonderful churches that we loved and served.

He was there at the weddings of our four children and, to date, three granddaughters.

He was there at the births of our nine wonderful grandchildren and, to date, seven marvelous great-grandchildren.

Yes, He has always been there, just like He promised!

Chapter 10

"*Behold* ... There is nothing too hard for You."

(Jeremiah 32:17)

"Ah, LORD, God! Behold, You have made the heavens
and the earth by Your great power and outstretched
arm. There is nothing too hard for You"
(Jeremiah 32:17).

Someone has said that there are thirty thousand
promises in God's Word. We can count on every one
of them, for God keeps His Word. Is there a problem in
your life right now that seems impossible to solve?

When I spoke at a retreat for ministers' wives,
I asked them to anonymously write on a card a deep
problem they had gone through or were currently
experiencing. On the next page are some of the problems
they wrote:

- Daughter in rehab for drugs and alcohol (third trip to rehab)
- Having been raped
- Eighteen-year-old daughter left home
- Family relationships
- Worldliness
- Disrespect to husband
- Impatience
- Unexpected death of husband
- Weight issues
- Death of two children
- Quick temper
- Loneliness
- Financial troubles
- Prayerlessness

Do you remember some of the monstrous problems in the Bible? God delivered everyone from these "impossible" situations.

- God parted the Red Sea, and His people walked through on dry ground (Exodus 14:29).
- Joshua led the Israelites to march around Jericho seven times and the walls came tumbling down (Joshua 6:15–16).

- Jesus called out, "Lazarus, come forth!" and he came back from the dead (John 11:43).
- Jesus took five loaves and two fishes and fed over five thousand people (Matthew 14:19).
- Jesus walked on the water and calmed the storm (Mark 6:48).
- Most of all, Jesus rose from the dead after three days and three nights (Matthew 27:63, 28:6).

Nothing, no nothing is too hard for God!

Does your problem seem like the Red Sea or the walls of Jericho? Your problem is not unique. Disease, death, and unfaithfulness have been around since the beginning of time. Remember that God destroyed the whole world because sin was so rampant.

There is one difference since the Flood. Jesus died, has risen from the dead, and conquered sin and the grave. We can bring our sins, our burdens, and our diseases and lay them down at Jesus' feet! He took our burdens upon Himself. He died our eternal death that we might have His eternal life.

> "For this God is our God for ever and ever: he will be our guide even unto death" (Psalm 48:14, KJV).

Chapter 11

"*Behold*, the virgin shall conceive . . ."

". . . Behold, the virgin shall conceive, and bear a Son,
and shall call His name Immanuel" (Isaiah 7:14b).

"'Behold, the virgin shall be with child, and shall bear a
Son, and they shall call His name Immanuel,' which is
translated, 'God with us'" (Matthew 1:23).

Unique for all time and eternity—the virgin birth.
No explanation except that it was an incomparable
miracle! Let us ask a couple of pertinent questions. First,
HOW?

How did the virgin birth occur? The angel Gabriel
explained it, "The Holy Spirit will come upon you . . ."
(Luke 1:35). Then one of the greatest statements of all
times says, "For with God nothing will be impossible"
(Luke 1:37).

But **WHY?** Why the virgin birth? It was essential! Evangelist John R. Rice put it this way, "To deny the virgin birth is to deny the deity of Christ, the inspiration of the Bible, the foundation of Christianity."[5] Sin was passed down through the blood of the man. The blood of Jesus was not tainted by sin because the blood of man did not enter the embryo. It was the blood of God—made possible by the virgin birth. The Holy Spirit overshadowed Mary and she became pregnant.

The virgin birth of Jesus was prophesied in Isaiah 7:14. How do we know this for sure? It is verified in the New Testament in Matthew 1:23. The Father of Jesus was not Joseph, but God Himself. Just think about that! Jesus bore witness to this fact many times.

- In the Temple when He was twelve years of age, Jesus questioned His parents, "Did you not know that I must be about My *Father's* business?" (Luke 2:49).
- He declared in John 10:30, "I and My *Father* are one."
- He taught His disciples to pray, "Our *Father,* which art in heaven . . ." (Matthew 6:9, KJV).

---

[5] John R. Rice, *The King of the Jews* (Murfreesboro, TN: Sword of the Lord Publishers, 1955), 35.

- "... for One is your *Father*, He who is in heaven" (Matthew 23:9).
- "The *Father* loves the Son ..." (John 3:35).
- "... but also said that God was His *Father*, making Himself equal with God" (John 5:18).
- "... we have one *Father*—God" (John 8:41).

Mary kept all these things and pondered them in her heart. Her Son, the Son of God?

There is an inspiring book written by a Muslim woman convert to Christ entitled *I Dared to Call Him Father!* Muslims have no concept of God as a father. They have no relationship with this God they call Allah.

Since childhood, I have called my God, "Father." What a privilege, what a joy! He is my Protector and my Provider. He has given to me a treasure book of great and precious promises. I can count on these promises to be true because He *is* the Truth.

He is faithful. I can count on Him at *all* times. He is the everlasting Father. He is Jehovah Shammah— my Lord Who is always there. My earthly father wasn't perfect, but he was a faithful provider and a protector to me. He was a man of integrity.

I am grateful for this heritage. But more than that, I am eternally grateful for a heavenly Father Who always keeps His Word. I can count on Him. He has promised to never leave me. My greatest possession is the promise of His presence. Adrian said, "God's promises are not mottos to hang on the wall. They are checks to take to the bank." I have claimed the promise of His constant presence. I am never lonely! My heavenly Father watches over me. He has promised, "The LORD shall preserve your going out and your coming in From this time forth, and even forevermore" (Psalm 121:8). He is my "Everlasting Father" (Isaiah 9:6c). And Jesus is Emmanuel—"God with us" (Matthew 1:23).

Chapter 12

Behold, the Greatest Gift

"Behold, the virgin shall conceive, and bear a son, and shall call His name Immanuel" (Isaiah 7:14b).

"For God so loved the world, that he **gave** his only begotten Son, that whosoever believeth in him should not perish, but have everlasting life" (John 3:16).

Behold, the Greatest Gift in all the world was given that first Christmas.

> He was the God-man
> God came down to earth
> As a man—a Jewish man (Isaiah 42:1–9)
> Yet He was God!

He came down that first Christmas to demonstrate His love.

This is love—
Not that we loved God
But that He loved us;
That He **gave** His only begotten Son
To be the substitute for our sins.
He loved so much that
He was wounded for our transgressions
He was bruised for our iniquities (Isaiah 53:5b)
The Lord laid on Him the sins of us all (Isaiah 53:6).

What was His name
    That One Who came
    Who came to earth on Christmas?

The prophet Isaiah said,

"For unto us a child is born,
Unto us a Son is given . . .
And His name will be called
Wonderful, Counselor,
Mighty God,
Everlasting Father,
Prince of Peace" (Isaiah 9:6).

"Behold, the virgin shall conceive
And bear a Son, and shall call
His name Immanuel" (Isaiah 7:14).
Which means, "God with us" (Matthew 1:23).

His earthly name was Jesus
Which means JEHOVAH SAVES!
　(Matthew 1:21).

For God so loved the world

He **gave**
He **gave** His Son
That whoever believes on Him
That whoever receives Him should
not perish
But have everlasting life (John 3:16).

That gift was love
That gift was life
That gift was light (John 1:4–9)

Some would not receive the gift

But whoever reaches out by faith
And takes the gift
May have eternal life.

Jesus is the gift—
Jesus is the gift of love!

He loved so much

That He died.
He died that we might live.

**But He was God—the One and only
  God-man. So . . .**

> He rose from the dead
> Now He lives on high;
> He still loves.

Behold, He is still the Greatest Gift!
  The Gift that came down to earth
  That first Christmas!

Chapter 13

"*Behold*, I will do a new thing,"

(Isaiah 43:19)

After Adrian had "graduated to glory," I had to learn to depend on my spiritual husband. I turned to His Word every day for guidance. This particular day I had been reading a familiar passage—one that I loved so much—"When thou passest through the waters, I will be with thee; and through the rivers, they shall not overflow thee: when thou walkest through the fire, thou shalt not be burned; neither shall the flame kindle upon thee" (Isaiah 43:2, KJV).

A friend whom I highly regarded, and also a widow, Vonette (Mrs. Bill) Bright, called to invite me to go with her to Korea to a historic women's prayer gathering. I was honored, but frankly, it was out of my comfort zone, and I simply said no. I have been to many places around the world with Adrian. But the thought of going without him didn't inspire me.

She asked me to reconsider, and I told her that I would talk to my children and see what they said. I was greatly surprised when they all encouraged me to go. I had left my Bible open on my vanity in my bathroom that morning. When I went back in the room, I "happened" to glance at a verse that I had not read that morning. It was verse 19 of Isaiah 43. It said, "Behold, I will do a new thing; now it shall spring forth; shall ye not know it? I will even make a way in the wilderness, and rivers in the desert" (KJV). I am not given to emotional experiences, but it was like I felt a burning sensation within me. I interpreted it to mean that God was telling me to go. So I called Vonette back and told her I would go with her.

Then I discovered a serious conflict. During the same time that I would be gone to Korea, the Mid America Baptist Theological Seminary would be dedicating a new school of preaching in honor of my husband, and I was supposed to be there. My children and others then agreed that the dedication was my top priority. Consequently, I did not go to Korea to the Women's Prayer Summit.

I had been so convinced that God had spoken to my heart from Isaiah 43:19—that God was going to do "a new thing" in my life. Later, as I reflected on this situation, I concluded that God *was* inwardly speaking to me. He *did* want to do a new thing in me. As I look back over the years since Adrian went home, I can see that God has taken me places I never dreamed I would go, to declare to many others that God was my "help for today and my hope for tomorrow" and that He would also be their help and hope (Psalm 146:5).

God has done a new thing in my life. He has taken away some of my fears and filled me with His confidence. I always love the words of Major Ian Thomas:

> I can't, He never said I could.
> He can, He always said He would.

Chapter 14

"*Behold*, it is I."

(Isaiah 52:6, KJV)

"Therefore my people shall know my name:
therefore they shall know in that day that I am he that
doth speak: behold, it is I" (Isaiah 52:6, KJV).

What a senseless sin it is to take God's name in vain. "... for the LORD will not hold him guiltless who takes His name in vain" (Exodus 20:7). But every day people take that name—that matchless name—and drag it though the mire. It used to be against the standard of broadcasting to use that name above all names in vain. But they have now lifted that ban. "They" think that it is all right to use His name meaninglessly. People don't understand what a serious sin this is, what a holy name His name is. I would no more take that holy name in a flippant way than to spit in the face of my God.

At the burning bush, Moses asked God what *name* he should tell the people when they asked who sent him. God told Moses to tell them, "I AM THAT I AM" sent you (Exodus 3:14, KJV). In the New Testament when Jesus told the Jews that ". . . before Abraham was, I AM" (John 8:58), they understood *what* He was saying. However, they did not *believe* Him. They took up stones to cast at Him and said that He was guilty of blasphemy, claiming to be equal with God.

The third commandment tells us that we are to honor His name. It says in Exodus 20: "You shall not take the name of the LORD your God in vain . . ." (Exodus 20:7a). In the book of Malachi, the Lord of hosts said that His name should be great among the nations (Malachi 1:11c). He told the religious leaders of that day that He would send a curse on them if they did not give glory to His name (Malachi 2:2).

I love the scripture in Malachi 3:16 that tells about a *book of remembrance* that was being written in the very presence of God that contained the names of those who gave reverence to God and thought upon His name. I want *my* name written in that book. Yes, my name *will* be written in that book because I love His name. I honor that name that is above every name. I love to meditate on His name.

God has a *primary* name that reveals His very essence—I AM. It shows His eternality. There is no other like Him! He has many descriptive names, but He has a unique name of relationship—*Father*. He is our heavenly *Father*. Muslims do not believe that God is a father; hence, He cannot have a son.

Jesus taught His disciples to pray like this: "Our Father, which art in heaven, Hallowed be thy name . . ." (Matthew 6:9a, KJV). How grateful I am that I can cry out to Him, "My *Father*!" and "My God!" He cares for me, protects, and provides for me! I call Him Father every day!

In the gospels, Jesus presents Himself on seven different occasions as the "I Am" God:

> I AM the bread of life (John 6:48).
> I AM the light of the world (John 9:5).
> I AM the door of the sheep (John 10:7).
> I AM the good shepherd (John 10:11).
> I AM the resurrection and the life (John 11:25).
> I AM the way, the truth, and the life (John 14:6).
> I AM the vine (John 15:5).

I have a *primary* name. It is Joyce. I also have many descriptive names—sweetheart, honey, darling, mother, mom, mama, sis, friend, etc. There is one huge difference. My primary name does not reveal my essence. I had a beginning. At my birth, my parents gave me a name. I am not eternal. I was not "in the beginning." It is only God Who can be the great I AM—with no beginning and no ending. No, I cannot explain or understand this. I am not God. I must only bow at His feet and thank Him that *He* is God—that He is in control of everything. I don't have to understand *What* or *Why*, but only to long to know *Who*.

It was Job who desperately sought after God. He wanted to know *where* he could find Him (Job 23:3). At first, it was not to know Him, but to ask Him why (Job 23:4, 7). He knew he was not deserving of everything bad that had happened to him. When Job finally had an encounter with God, God asked Job *where* was he when the world was created and who did he think he was to question Him (Job 38:4). It was then and only then that Job laid down his questions and sought only to know *Who* God was. It was then sufficient to know Him. Job has been one of my greatest counselors. He has helped me to lay aside the *why* question and to major on *Who* God is (Job 42:5).

I love His descriptive names; they have helped me to know *Who* He is. As a widow, He is my spiritual Husband—the One Who protects me. That name is Jehovah Sabaoth—The Lord of hosts. I have cried out to Him many times and asked Him to "fight my battles" for me. When I am in need, He is Jehovah Jireh—my Provider. When I am troubled, He is Jehovah Shalom—my Peace. When I am ill, He is Jehovah Rapha—my

Healer. When I feel defeated, He is Jehovah Nissi—my Victory. And my favorite Old Testament name is Jehovah Shammah—My Lord Who is always there. I could go on and on to tell you what He means to me and what He has done for me as expressed in His names. I encourage you to know His names and with them, cry out to Him in your need.

My favorite name of all, the New Testament name for God, that name that is above every name, that name to Whom every knee shall bow and every tongue shall confess that He is Lord—is Jesus! His name means Jehovah saves. The gospel of Matthew adds, ". . . for He will save His people from their sins" (Matthew 1:21). Yes, He is Lord. But more than that, He is *my* Lord! I have bowed before Him and confessed that there is no other like Him—no name like His name. Won't you acknowledge Him as *your* Lord?

Oh, how I love the name of Jesus. One of my very favorite pastimes is to sing about that name. I collect songs about that wonderful name. My all-time favorite song about His name is "There's Something About That Name" by Bill and Gloria Gaither.[6] I first heard that simple but profound song at a women's retreat. I fell in love with it. I shared it with our minister of music,

---

[6] William and Gloria Gaither, *Glorious (Christ for the Nations)*, "There's Something About That Name," © 1970 William J. Gaither, Inc. ARR UBP of Gaither Copyright Management.

Jim Whitmire. He had never heard it. It became *my* song. When we went to a new church in 1972—Bellevue Baptist Church in Memphis, Tennessee—no one had ever heard that song, that song with a haunting melody and gripping words. Since then, this simple song has gone around the world, and it seems like everyone knows it and has been blessed by its message—the message about that name, which is above every name.

Adrian used to say, "I just love the way the name Jesus fits on my tongue." Indeed, "Jesus, Jesus, Jesus, there's something about that name!"

"But as many as received Him, to them He gave the right to become children of God, to those who believe in His *name*" (John 1:12, emphasis added).

> ". . . there is no other *name* under heaven given among men by which we must be saved" (Acts 4:12).

> ". . . that signs and wonders may be done through the *name* of Your holy Servant Jesus" (Acts 4:30).

> "And whatever you do in word or deed, do all in the *name* of the Lord Jesus, giving thanks to God the Father through Him" (Colossians 3:17).

"He was clothed with a robe dipped in blood, and His *name* is called The Word of God" (Revelation 19:13).

"And He has on His robe and on His thigh a *name* written: KING OF KINGS AND LORD OF LORDS" (Revelation19:16).

We are told to pray in Jesus' name. "If ye shall ask any thing in my *name*, I will do it" (John 14:14, KJV). His name is to be honored and to be praised. We are commanded numerous times to *sing* praises to His name.

"I will praise the *name* of God with a song . . ." (Psalm 69:30).

"In God we boast all day long, And praise Your *name* forever. Selah" (Psalm 44:8).

"I will be glad and rejoice in You; I will sing praise to Your *name*, O Most High" (Psalm 9:2).

"So will I sing praise unto Your *name* forever . . ." (Psalm 61:8).

Jesus, oh how sweet the name
Jesus, every day the same
Jesus, let all saints proclaim
Its worthy praise forever![7]

"Behold, it is I!"

---

[7] W. C. Martin, "The Name of Jesus Is So Sweet," 1901. Public domain.

Chapter 15

"*Behold* your son! . . . Behold your mother!"
(John 19:26–27)

"*Behold*, the maidservant of the Lord!" (Luke 1:38a).

Jesus highly regarded His mother. Even when He was on the cross, He provided for the care of His mother, asking His "beloved disciple," John, to be like a son to His mother. I, too, highly regard Mary, the mother of Jesus. She was a wonderful example of godly and immediate submission. There is much about her that I would like to emulate. What a woman she must have been! However, I do not adhere to the false doctrines that surround her life. For many years, I have been attracted to this most highly favored woman (Luke 1:28).

> She was a woman chosen by God
> to actually conceive the Son of God
> to bear the Son of man
> to cradle Him in her arms

to nurture and train Him
and then
to give Him up to the whole world.

When Mary and Jesus' brothers tried to see Him (Mark 3:31–35) He asked, "Who is My mother, or My brothers? . . . *For whoever does the will of God* is My brother and My sister and mother" (emphasis added). In other words, Jesus did not see Mary as spiritually superior and set apart from other believers. She was His *earthly* mother. She was not without sin. She confessed Jesus as her Savior (Luke 1:47).

The angel did not say, "Mary, you are sinless," but only, "You have found favor with God." She was not to be called the highest, but her virgin-born Son would be called the "Son of the Highest." Mary is not the bride— the church is called "the bride of Christ." She is only a part of the bride.

Why do you think she so easily received God's Word to her? I believe that she had a *prepared heart*. Luke 1:28 and 30 say that she was "highly favored." I like what the center column reference in my Bible says this means, "graciously accepted." God had been observing Mary.

He *knew* who she was.
He called her name.
He knew *what* she was.
He *knew* she was a virgin.

The influence of Mary will be felt through all eternity. How grateful I am that a young virgin maiden had so prepared her heart that she heard God's Word and that she believed God's Word. I want to be one of the "whoevers"—whoever does the will of the Father. I hope that you do too!

A Small Intruder

No wedding feast
No loved ones gathered;
No friends to laugh and sing
Instead an angel's greeting,

"You're special, Mary
You'll be the mother of the King.

No honeymoon, no ecstasy
Of young love's sweet demand
Instead a quiet questioning:
'How can this be when
I know not a man?'"

Not much time alone with Joseph
To plan, to dream, to love
Instead a "small Intruder"
Sent with a message from above.

No sad disappointment
But His divine appointment
With young Mary, lass of Galilee;
Instead a dedication
And a joyful adoration
"Here, Lord, is my availability!"

Mary said, "Behold the maidservant of the Lord! Let it be to me according to your word" (Luke 1:38a). May we learn from her attitude of immediate submission. For Mary, who believed God's promises, came the day when the "performance" was accomplished.

"Blessed is she who believed, for there will be a fulfillment of those things which were told her from the Lord" (Luke 1:45).

And indeed there was! One *silent night* in the little town of Bethlehem a baby was born.

A Baby—A Baby was born!
He would save His people
from their sins.

A Baby—A Baby was born!
But He was *born to die*
for the sins of all mankind.

Yes, Jesus was the Savior of Mary. He is *my* Savior. He will be your Savior too. Simply ask Him!

Chapter 16

"*Behold*, I bring you good tidings . . ."
(Luke 2:10)

The Angels Looked Down

The *angels* looked down with great joy
Beholding the King become a babe;
They had **beheld** His glory with the Father
Now they **beheld** His suffering as a man
Not just any man
But the God-man!

They rejoiced at His birth
Came to Him after He had fasted
Forty days and nights
In the wilderness.

They ministered to Him in dark Gethsemane;
In the midst of His intense agony
They strengthened Him.

An *angel* rolled away the stone,
And two *angels* greeted Mary saying,
"He is not here, He is risen,
even as He said!"

When He ascended into heaven two *angels*
Stood by them and said,
"Why do you gaze into heaven?
This same Jesus will come again in the same way
As you have seen Him be taken into heaven."

Yes, He's coming back again!
The Lord Himself shall descend
With a shout
With the voice of an *archangel*
With the trump of God.
This One Who left His Father's glory
Will come in the glory of His Father
With His *angels*.

The *angels* rejoice at *our* salvation
Though they never knew this joy.
The *angels* are also sent to us
To protect and
To lead us safely home.

Home—in the presence of the Father,
The Son and the Holy Spirit;
Home—rejoicing *with* the *angels*
At the joy that our salvation brings.

Chapter 17

"*Behold*, we are going up to Jerusalem,"
(Luke 18:31)

When Jesus was twelve years old, He and His parents "went up to Jerusalem . . ." (Luke 2:42). He lingered behind in the Temple, "sitting in the midst of the teachers, both listening to them and asking them questions" (Luke 2:46).

It was here in Jerusalem that Jesus first acknowledged His unique calling and relationship to His heavenly Father. "And he said to them, 'Why did you seek Me? Did you not know that I must be about my Father's business?'" (Luke 2:49).

Jesus had visited Jerusalem a number of times. But now it was that "appointed time." Jesus began to show His disciples that He must go to Jerusalem "and suffer . . . and be killed, and be raised the third day" (Matthew 16:21). Three times He told them what "going up to Jerusalem" would mean. However, they did not comprehend His prophetic words. It was as if there was a veil over their understanding.

What did Jesus *do* when He came to Jerusalem?

- First, as Jesus drew near the city of Jerusalem, He wept over it (Luke 19:41). He then predicted the destruction of this beautiful city (Luke 19:43–44).
- Next, He rode into the city on a lowly donkey as the people hailed Him as their king (Matthew 21:7).
- He saw the corruption of those who bought and sold in the temple area, and He entered the courtyard and cleansed the temple by knocking over all the tables and merchants (Matthew 21:12).
- Then He taught the people as He had done on many occasions (Matthew 21:23).
- Finally, He was crucified there— outside the city walls of Jerusalem (Matthew 27:35).

"Behold, we are going up to Jerusalem" (Luke 18:31).

Chapter 18

"*Behold!* The Lamb . . ."
(John 1:29)

The *picture* of the lamb is central to the Bible. Jesus came to be baptized by John the Baptist and John declared, "Behold! The Lamb of God who takes away the sin of the world!" (John 1:29).

We can trace the history of the lamb throughout the whole Bible. Take a look with me at the story behind the lamb.

Behold, the Lamb

"Behold! The *Lamb* of God
Who takes away the sin of the world!" (John 1:29).

Isaac asked, "My father . . . where is the *lamb*?"
Abraham replied,
"God will provide Himself a *Lamb*"
(Genesis 22:7–8, KJV).

The blood of the Passover *lamb* was shed
And placed upon the doorposts of each house
So the death angel would pass over (Exodus 12:7).

Year after year the *lambs* were slain,
The blood was spilled;
Surely, the people would know when John cried out,
"Behold! The *Lamb* of God!"

This is My body, broken for you.
This is my blood; drink all of it! (Matthew 26:26–28).
But they didn't "see."
They didn't understand (Luke 24:8).

He was brought as a *lamb* to the slaughter,
And as a *lamb* before her shearers was silent (Isaiah 53:7).
So He opened not His mouth;
"He answered him nothing" (Luke 23:9).

He never defended Himself,
Though sinless, He was guilty;
Because He took upon Himself my sin, your sin!

And at the moment the High Priest slew the *lamb*
The veil to the Holy of Holies was torn;
The *Lamb* of God cried out, "It is finished!"
(Luke 23:45).

Behold the *Lamb*, the *Lamb* of God,
Who has taken away the sin of the world!

His blood was shed upon the cross that day;
The spotless, sinless *Lamb* was slain (John 2:34).
He took my place.
I was the guilty one,
He bore my sin away
As far as the east is from the west! (Psalm 103:12).

This spotless *Lamb* was slain but is no longer dead;
On the third day He rose again
Just as He said (Luke 24:34).

Their "eyes" were opened;
It was Jesus, precious *Lamb* of God,
Behold the *Lamb*!
Slain from the foundation of the world
(Revelation 13:8).

He ascended to His Father (Acts 1:9)
Is seated there upon the throne
The Father and the *Lamb* (Revelation 5:13).

There was a great multitude
Standing before the throne;
And in front of the *Lamb*.
They were wearing white robes

And holding palm branches
In their hands.
They cried with a loud voice,
"Salvation belongs to our God
Who sits on the throne,
And to the Lamb!" (Revelation 7:9–10).

The saints fell down before Him
And cried out, "Worthy is the *Lamb*
Who was slain
To receive power and riches
And wisdom, And strength
And honor and glory and blessing!"
Behold the *Lamb*!

The accuser of the brethren was cast down
(Revelation 14:10),
And these overcame Him by the blood of the *Lamb*
(Revelation 12:10).

And the overcomers were given harps by God,
And they sang the song of the Lamb,
"Great and marvelous are Your works,
Lord God Almighty!
Just and true are Your ways" (Revelation 15:3).

And look, behold, the Bridegroom comes
to claim His bride
Her garments are made white in the blood of the *Lamb*!
(Revelation 7:14).
And here comes the bride—the bride of Christ!
The church of the living God (Revelation 19:7).

The Marriage Supper has been prepared,
The Marriage Supper of the *Lamb* (Revelation 19:9);
And there I am—seated by His side;
I am a part of the Bride of Christ!
I have been made ready,
Arrayed in white linen,
Clean and white.
I am washed in the blood of the *Lamb*!
(Revelation 19:8).

And my new name is written there
There in the *Lamb's* Book of Life!
(Revelation 20:15, 21:27).
I am not worthy;
I am there because of Him!
Behold the *Lamb*!
Seated on the throne with His Father (Revelation 22:3).

I'm in my new home
This is heaven at last!

No need for a temple,
For the Lord God Almighty and the *Lamb*
Are the temple of it (Revelation 21:22).

No need for the sun or moon
For the *Lamb* is the light thereof (Revelation 21:23).
He showed me a pure river of water of life,
Clear as crystal—pouring forth
Out of the throne of God and
Of the *Lamb* (Revelation 22:1).

And best of all—
There shall be no more curse
But the throne of God and of the *Lamb*
Shall be in it,
And His servants shall serve Him
And we shall see His face! (Revelation 22:3–4).

"Face to face with Christ, my Savior,
Face to face, what will it be,
When with rapture I behold Him,
Jesus Christ Who died for me?"[8]

Behold the *Lamb*, the *Lamb* of God
Who takes away the sin of the world!

---

[8] Carrie E. Breck, "Face to Face with Christ, My Savior,"
1898. Public domain.

Chapter 19

"*Behold*, the Man!"

(John 19:5)

When Jesus came to earth,
He laid aside His glory;

Some saw Him as a man
A friend
A son
A brother.

Others saw Him as a special man
With power to cast out demons
To even raise the dead,

But they didn't see His glory;
For when He came to earth
He laid it all aside.

He came to live a sinless life
And then to sacrifice that life,

That I might know eternal life
That I might know Him,
The Giver of all life.

Then when His plan was finished
He asked His Father
For His glory to be seen again;
That all might see the oneness
With His Father.

Oh, the glory laid aside
Once shared with His Father
Would be His again—
Displayed for all to see
And every knee shall bow
Every tongue confess that
Jesus Christ is Lord.

By one man's disobedience
Many were made sinners,
So by the obedience of "one Man"
Shall many be made righteous.

Yes, I see "one Man" hanging on a cross
Shedding His blood
Giving His life.
He Who knew no sin, becoming sin for me,
"One Man," but more than a man.

This "one Man" offered up one sacrifice
This "one Man" freely gave one offering
To perfect those who believe forever.
I see "one Man" hanging on a cross.

His name is Jesus
Sinless, spotless
Son of Man and Son of God.
Behold the God-Man!
"One Man," but more, much more than a man.

Chapter 20

"*Behold,* two men stood by them . . ."
(Luke 24:4)

_____

While standing inside the rock-hewn empty tomb, where many Christians believe that Jesus rose from the dead, our group sang,

> He is Lord, He is Lord
> He is risen from the dead
> And He is Lord,
> Every knee shall bow
> Every tongue confess
> That Jesus Christ is Lord.

It was a stirring experience because it reminded me of that day when Jesus came out of the tomb and has been alive forevermore. I personally believe that this was *the place*—the place where He rose from the dead. But whether this is the literal place or not isn't important. The life-transforming truth is that He *is* alive—alive in me and

He can be alive in you, if you believe that He died, was buried, and rose again and confess that He is Lord!

I have returned to this place many times. It is my favorite place in all of the Holy Land. There's a beautiful garden here, kept by faithful Christians. It is a quiet place in the midst of the hustle and bustle of tourists and those who have come to shop in the old city of Jerusalem, which is right across the street. There is a busy bus station nearby at the foot of a hill—a rugged hill that many believe is the hill of Calvary. It is a haven where you can hear the birds singing, as you are still and wait on God to meet you there.

Oh, He can meet you anywhere—right here, right now. I love to take time to sit and meditate about what took place here over two thousand years ago. But whether you ever get to go to *this* place is irrelevant. You can read the story from God's Word for yourself. You can travel there in your spiritual imagination. But praise God, He isn't there anymore! He is alive. He has risen from the dead, and He is alive!

Chapter 21

"*Behold*, now is the day of salvation."

(2 Corinthians 6:2)

The 4th Station of the Cross

As our group walked along a street in Old Jerusalem, a man came out of a shop and said that he recognized my husband's voice. He had been listening to the program *Love Worth Finding*, of which my husband was the international speaker.

We paused and someone in our group took a picture of my husband and that man. Later, that person in our group sent me a copy of that picture. In the upper left-hand corner of the picture was the name of that shop in Arabic and in English.

Now it was twelve years later, my husband had died four years previously, and I was again walking through the streets of Old Jerusalem with a group from my church. A friend, Riad Saba, who was a Christian Arab, was with our small group. We had a "free day" in

Jerusalem, and we were going into the marketplace in Old Jerusalem. Riad, who spoke Arabic as well as English, said that he would help me find the shop. Someone had told me that he knew that man and that he had been very ill for two years. I thought that perhaps someone in the shop would take the picture to him.

When we found the shop, someone there told us to go to "the fourth station of the cross." (Religious "pilgrims" follow the "stations of the cross" along what is known as the Via Dolorosa—the way of the cross.)

The man told Riad that we would find a juice shop there and that someone in that shop would be able to tell us about the man in the picture. We found the fourth station of the cross, and my friend Riad went into the shop and showed the picture. The man's grown son came out and said, "There comes my father now!"

There he was, the man in the picture! His name was Nasser Basti. It was obvious that he was not well. He wheezed when he talked. He was wearing a wool cap over his ears, and he looked much older. We hugged. They invited Riad and me to have a cup of tea at their outdoor café. I gave him the picture and recalled the story of a number of years earlier. He remembered and said, "It was twelve years ago."

We drank our tea, took pictures, and shared how he could still watch and hear my husband on TV and the Internet. We exchanged e-mail addresses. I had put a copy of the picture in a plastic bag, along with a copy of "The Four Spiritual Laws" tract and the name and address of our ministry.

I encouraged him to put his trust in the Lord and to watch the *Love Worth Finding* program. We hugged again and said goodbye. I don't think it was just by chance that I found that man again—at the fourth station of the cross.

"Behold . . . now is the day of salvation" (2 Corinthians 6:2).

Chapter 22

Behold, what manner of love . . ."
(1 John 3:1)

"Behold what manner of love the Father has bestowed
on us, that we should be called children
of God!" (1 John 3:1a).

What kind of love is this?

It is undeserved!
It is sacrificial!
It is marvelous!

Just think about it! We who are believers in Christ
are called the *children of God*. That means that I am a child
of the King. We sang this song when I was young:

A Child of the King

My Father is rich in houses and lands
He holdeth the wealth of the world

In His hands;
Of rubies and diamonds
Of silver and gold
His coffers are full
He has riches untold.

My Father's own Son,
The Savior of men,
Once wandered on earth
As the poorest of them;
But now He is reigning
Forever on high,
And will give me a home
In heav'n by and by.

I'm a child of the King
A child of the King
With Jesus my Savior
I'm a child of the King.[9]

---

[9] Harriet E. Buell, "A Child of the King," 1877, public domain.

Probably the greatest words ever penned on the love of God are these:

The Love of God

The love of God is greater far
Than tongue or pen can ever tell;
It goes beyond the highest star,
And reaches to the lowest hell.
The guilty pair bowed down with care,
God gave His Son to win;
His erring child He reconciled,
And pardoned from his sin.

Could we with ink the ocean fill,
And were the skies of parchment made
Were every stalk on earth a quill,
And every man a scribe by trade,
To write the love of God above
Would drain the ocean dry,
Nor could the scroll contain the whole,
Tho' stretched from sky to sky.

O love of God, how rich and pure!
How measureless and strong!
It shall forevermore endure
The saints and angels song.[10]

---

[10] F. M. Lehman, "The Love of God," 1917, public domain.

What kind of love is this? It's a "so-that" love: "For God *so* loved the world, *that* he gave his only begotten Son, that whosoever believeth in him should not perish, but have everlasting life" (John 3:16, KJV).

He gave His most priceless treasure that we might be a part of His family. Gloria and Bill Gaither put it well in their "homey" song, "The Family of God."[11] Yes, we are joint heirs with Jesus! I can never stop praising Him for His love.

We usually think of 1 Corinthians 13 as the *love chapter* in the Bible. But 1 John 3 and 4 and 1 John 5:1–3 are equally "love chapters." They tell of God's love for us and of our love for Him. But they go further. 1 John 4:11 says, "Beloved, if God so loved us, we ought also to love another."

Open your Bible to 1 John 3 and begin reading. Everywhere you see the word *love* draw a little heart around it. Then take a red pencil and shade it in red to represent His blood—the spilled blood of Jesus—the evidence of this love! Yes, ". . . God *is* love, and he who abides in love abides in God, and God in him" (1 John 4:16b, emphasis added).

"We love Him because He first loved us" (1 John 4:19).

"Behold what manner of love the Father has bestowed on us, that we should be called children of God!" (1 John 3:1a).

---

[11] William Gaither, "The Family of God," 1970.

Chapter 23

"*Behold,* two of them were traveling . . . to a village called Emmaus . . ."

(Luke 24:13–14)

"Now behold, two of them were traveling that same day to a village called Emmaus . . . and they talked together of all *these things* which had happened" (Luke 24:13–14, emphasis added).

These Things

Behold, two forlorn disciples walked
The Emmaus Road that day,
The day that Christ rose from the dead.
As they talked and reasoned
About *these things,*
Jesus Himself drew near, but
They didn't recognize Who He was.

"What *things* are you talking about?" Jesus asked.

They said, "Haven't you heard
How they condemned and crucified
Jesus of Nazareth?
We believed He was to be our redeemer,
But today is the third day
Since *these things* were done.
Some say He is alive,
But we do not know *these things* for sure."

Then Jesus said,
"Oh, if you had known the scriptures,
You would have known that Christ
Would suffer and rise again."
Then He explained in Moses and all
The prophets *these things*
About Himself.

"Stay with us tonight," they pleaded,
"And tell us more."
And so He tarried and blessed and broke
The bread at suppertime that night.

As He broke the bread their
Eyes were opened—
It was Jesus Himself!
But then He vanished out of
Their sight.

They said one to another,
"Did not our hearts burn within us
While He talked with us—
As He opened the scriptures
Along the way?"

These things were all concerning Him!
He is in all the scriptures—
In every book
On almost every page.

When I was in the Holy Land, I wanted so much to go to the *place* that many believe were the ruins of the Road to Emmaus. I wanted to read the story of how Jesus Himself drew near and went with those two grieving disciples. I wanted to remember that moment when "their eyes were opened" and they knew Him.

Don't you wish you knew what He taught them "along the way"—that seven mile Bible conference? What a revelation, as He opened to them the scriptures—beginning at Moses, then all of the prophets and the Psalms. My favorite book in all of the Bible is the book of Psalms. I would have loved to have heard every single word about Jesus there in that wonderful book.

Just think—Jesus is in all of the scriptures. Why wasn't it recorded? What did He tell them that day? It is only my opinion, but I believe that He wants you and me to walk with Him day by day as He points out Himself to us personally in all of His Word, showing us where He is in the figures, the types.

It is always a thrill as I discover another treasure from His Word about Himself. Come with me on this spiritual journey as day by day, step by step He reveals Who He is through *our* daily experiences. Then we, too, can say along with those two disciples on the Road to Emmaus when their eyes were opened, "He is risen, indeed!"

I remember singing this old hymn when I was just a child. These words are a passionate prayer:

Open My Eyes, That I May See

Open my eyes, that I may see
Glimpses of truth Thou hast for me;
Place in my hands the wonderful key
That shall unclasp and set me free.

Silently now, I wait for Thee,
Ready my God, Thy will to see,
Open my eyes, illumine me,
Spirit divine![12]

"Open thou mine eyes, that I may **behold** wondrous things out of thy law" (Psalm 119:18, KJV, emphasis added).

---

[12] Clara H. Scott, "Open My Eyes, That I May See," 1895, public domain.

Chapter 24

"*Behold*, the tabernacle of God is with men,"

(Revelation 21:3)

———————————

One day there will be a *new* Jerusalem! John saw in a vision the holy city, *new* Jerusalem, coming down out of heaven from God, prepared as a bride adorned for her husband. A loud voice from heaven declared, "Behold, the tabernacle of God is with men, and He will dwell with them, and they shall be His people. God Himself will be with them and be their God" (Revelation 21:3).

Oh, what a day that will be! Heaven "come down to earth" will be a glorious place. There will be no more death, nor sorrow, nor crying. There shall be no more pain. God declared, "Behold, I make all things new" (Revelation 21:5). Just imagine, everything brand new!

There will be no more temple there, for the Lord God Almighty and the Lamb *is* its temple. There will be no need for the sun or the moon—for the glory of God illuminates it. The Lamb is its light (Revelation 21:22–23).

But the greatest thing about heaven is that we shall see His face (Revelation 22:4). We shall *behold* Him. As Roy and Revel Hession say, "It is enough to see Jesus and to go on seeing Him."[13] We will be "looking unto Jesus, the author and finisher of our faith, who for the joy that was set before Him endured the cross, despising the shame, and has sat down at the right hand of the throne of God" (Hebrews 12:2).

We do not know what God the Father looks like, for He is spirit. There are promises throughout the Bible, however, that one day we shall see His face. Psalm 17:15 says, "As for me, I will *behold* thy face in righteousness: I shall be satisfied, when I awake, with thy likeness" (KJV, emphasis added).

"Philip said to Him, 'Lord, show us the Father, and it is sufficient for us'" (John 14:8). Jesus indeed came to show us the Father. He said, "He who has seen Me has seen the Father" (John 14:9). We do not know what the Father *looks* like, but we can know what He *is* like.

> God is loving
> He is compassionate
> He is righteous

---

[13] Roy Hession and Revel Hession, *We Would See Jesus* (Ft. Washington, PA: CLC Ministries, 2005).

He is just
He is forgiving.

He loves beauty
He loves color
He loves design
He loves variety
He loves me.

One day we will see the Father *and* the Son. Revelation tells us, "They shall see His face . . ." (Revelation 22:4a). Oh, what joy!

I love that old hymn, "Face to Face with Christ, My Savior." I just sang it recently at the memorial service of one of my best friends, Mary Buckner. Before Mary went to heaven, we talked a lot about what heaven will be like. But to see His face will be beyond description!

Yes, heaven is a wonderful place! I want to go there. I want to see Jesus most of all. But I want to see *you* there. Yes, together, we shall behold Him!

My Forever Home

I'm going home
To live with Him forever;
My Lord, my Shepherd
And my Friend.

What a joyful welcome
There will be;
With loved ones gathered
And Jesus by their side.

He'll reach to wipe the
Teardrops from my eyes;
No more crying here—
No more pain, or death or sorrow (Revelation 21:4).

Just listen to the choir,
There's a place saved just for you;
We've been practicing for ages
For the marriage of the Lamb.

Come, sing honor and praises unto Him!
You'll notice there's no temple here; (Revelation 21:22)
The Lord God Almighty
And the Lamb
Are all the temple needed.

This city needs no sun,
No moon to shine at night;
For there shall be no night in
My forever home (Revelation 21:23, 25).

The Lord God will be the Light
In this city so fair; (Revelation 22:5)
The gates are always open wide
To welcome those to soon arrive.

A river of pure water will be
Flowing there to drink; (Revelation 22:1)
Trees with leaves for healing (Revelation 22:2)
Will line the street, paved with purest gold.

There'll be no curse there in that place,
No sin allowed to enter in;
A wall of jasper, great and high, (Revelation 21:18)
Gates of pearl, foundations laid with precious stones
(Revelation 21:19, 21).

This is Paradise!
The home I've longed for,
Dreamed of all my life.
Yes, I'm going home
To live with Him forever.

He's my Shepherd,
He's my Lamb—
Son of God and Son of Man;
Sent to guide me
Sent to bear my sin

And take my place;
Sent to lead me safely home.

"Behold, the tabernacle of God is with men"
(Revelation 21:3).

Chapter 25

"*Behold*, I am coming quickly,"

(Revelation 22:12)

Who said these stirring words? In verse 13, He identifies Himself. "I am the Alpha and the Omega, the Beginning and the End, the First and the Last." In verse 16, He gets more specific. "I Jesus, have sent My angel to testify to you these things in the churches. I am the Root and Offspring of David, the Bright and Morning Star."

Yes, it is Jesus Who is coming and when He does, He will come quickly. I've stood on the Mount of Olives many times and led our group in singing this simple song that assures us of His coming, and I've wondered, *Could this be the very time of His return today—right now?*

> Coming again, coming again
> May be morning, may be noon
> May be evening and may be soon;
> Coming again, coming again

> Oh, what a wonderful day it will be
> Jesus is coming again![14]

He will bring a reward with Him. Revelation tells us that we will be judged for our works to receive a reward. "Blessed is he who keeps the words of the prophecy of this book. . . . And behold, I am coming quickly, and My reward is with Me, to give to every one according to his work" (Revelation 22:7, 12).

When He ascended into heaven after His resurrection, ". . . two men stood by them in white apparel, who also said, 'Men of Galilee, why do you stand gazing up into heaven? This same Jesus, who was taken up from you into heaven, will so come in like manner as you saw Him go into heaven'" (Acts 1:10b–11).

Yes, this same Jesus will come again! And He will bring His reward with Him. He could come at any moment, like a thief in the night (Revelation 3:3). Oh, I want to be ready. I want to be an overcomer who will walk with Jesus in white garments (Revelation 3:4–5).

I want my name written in the Book of Life, for He will confess my name before His Father and before His angels (Revelation 3:5). I am anticipating the day when the sky shall split and Jesus will come again.

---

[14] Words and music by John W. Peterson, "Jesus Is Coming Again," © 1957 by John W. Peterson Music Co. All rights reserved.

The book of Zechariah tells of that day, the day of the Lord. "Behold the day of the LORD is coming . . . And in that day His feet will stand on the Mount of Olives, Which faces Jerusalem on the east. And the Mount of Olives shall be split in two . . ." (Zechariah 14:1, 4).

"And in that day it shall be That living waters shall flow from Jerusalem . . . and the LORD shall be King over all the earth. In that day it shall be 'The LORD is one,' and His name is one" (Zechariah 14:8–9).

I have sung this gospel song many times. It is my earnest prayer!

> Come on down, Lord Jesus
> And take us away
> Come on down, Lord Jesus
> Could this be the day?[15]

> "Even so, come, Lord Jesus"
> (Revelation 22:20).

---

[15] Jack Hayford, "Come on Down," 1974 © Mandina Music.

Closing

"When I *behold* You there upon that cruel cross,"

_____

What a blessing it has been for me to behold my God:

> in creation
> in the burning bush
> in the "city of our God"—Jerusalem
> at the cross
> at the empty tomb
> on the Road to Emmaus
> in the new Jerusalem!

When I *behold* you there upon that cruel cross,
I wonder why, oh why were You hanging there?
Was it because of those who hated and
Despised Your blameless life,

Because of those who nailed you to the cross,
Or was it because of me and for all my sins?

When I look into Your face, I know the reason
Why You were hanging there—

Your piercing eyes look deep within my soul;
It was for me and for my sins
You hung upon that cross.
I know You took my place
Showed me your amazing grace
And I'm more than sorry for all my sins,
For all the pain and guilt You bore for me.

I lay my life down at Your feet
A new life to begin;
I turn from my way to follow only You.

When I behold You there upon that cross
I'm more than sorry.
I'm changed, cleansed by Your blood;
I'm now brand new.

***

I invite you now to kneel with me at the foot
of the cross—to confess with your mouth that Jesus is

Lord. To believe in your heart that God has raised Him from the dead (Romans 10:9–10). To yield your life to Him as I have done.

Kneel at the Cross

Kneel at the cross
Christ will meet you there
Come while He waits for you
Listen to His voice, leave with Him your cares
And begin life anew.

Kneel at the cross, kneel at the cross
Leave every care, leave every care.
Kneel at the cross, kneel at the cross
Jesus will meet you there.
—anonymous

Appendix

I taught a children's new members' class for over forty years. The first lesson was always about the meaning of salvation. There are many meaningful "plans" to teach salvation. I always used what has commonly been called *The Roman Road to Salvation.* I don't know who originally came up with this idea. Ruth Ann Shelton has drawn this rendition of *The Roman Road* that I used with the children for many years. I present it here for you to consider if you have never been saved. "Behold, now is the day of salvation" (2 Corinthians 6:2b). Won't you turn from your sin and receive Him as the Lord of your life?

The Roman Road to Salvation

1. All have sinned.

> ". . . for all have sinned and fall short of the glory of God . . ." (Romans 3:23).

2. **The wages of sin is death. The gift of God is eternal life.**

> "For the wages of sin is death,
> but the gift of God is eternal life in Christ Jesus our
> Lord" (Romans 6:23).

3. **God showed His love for us and although we are sinners, Christ died for us.**

> "But God demonstrates His own love toward us,
> in that while we were still sinners, Christ
> died for us" (Romans 5:8).

4. **To be saved you must confess with your mouth that Jesus is Lord and believe with your heart that God raised Him from the dead.**

> "If you confess with your mouth the Lord Jesus and
> believe in your heart that God has raised Him from the
> dead, you will be saved. For with the heart one believes
> unto righteousness, and with the mouth confession is
> made unto salvation" (Romans 10:9–10).

5. **Everyone who calls on the name of God will be saved.**

> "For 'whoever calls on the name of the Lord
> shall be saved'" (Romans 10:13).

The Roman Road to Salvation

JESUS
Eternal Life in Heaven

5. Romans 10:13

4. Romans 10:9-10

3. Romans 5:8

2. Romans 6:23

1. Romans 3:23